TORTOISES
AT THE ZOO

written and photographed
by
Mia Coulton

Look at the big rock

in the water.

Oh, my!

It's not a rock, it's a tortoise!

It's a **giant** tortoise at the zoo.

A tortoise is a turtle, but a turtle is not always a tortoise.

The tortoise has a hard **she**ll.

The shell protects the tortoise from harm.

The tortoise has short thick legs that hold up its heavy body. Its elephant-like feet help the tortoise walk in the sand.

The tortoise does not have teeth, but its **jaw** has sharp edges that help **mash** its food.

A giant tortoise is one of the longest living animals on earth.

A giant tortoise can live for over 100 years.

Aldabra Tortoise

Glossary

giant: Being of great size

jaw: The upper and lower bony parts of the mouth

mash: To soften by crushing

shell: A hard, rigid covering